EXAMINING
AIRPLANE CRASHES

BY ANDREW HATCH

CLARA
HOUSE
BOOKS

First published in 2015 by Clara House Books, an imprint of
The Oliver Press, Inc.

Clara House Books
5707 West 36th Street
Minneapolis, MN 55416
USA

Editors: Mirella Miller and Arnold Ringstad
Series Designer: Maggie Villaume

Picture Credits
Kyodo News/AP Images, cover, 1; AP Images, 4, 6; Senee Sriyota/Shutterstock Images, 8; U.S. Federal Aviation Administration, 10; Thinkstock, 12, 26; Patricia Soon/Thinkstock, 14; U.S. Air Force, 17, 28–29; Jeff Gross/Thinkstock, 18; Dorling Kindersley/Thinkstock, 21; Howard Castleberry/Houston Chronicle/AP Images, 22; Steven Day/AP Images, 24–25; Maxim Zmeyev/Reuters/Corbis, 31; Master Sgt. William Greer/U.S. Air Force, 33; Michel Euler/AP Images, 34; Staff Sgt. Samuel Morse/U.S. Air Force, 37; Staff Sgt. Vernon Young Jr./U.S. Air Force, 39; Airman 1st Class Ryan Callaghan/U.S. Air Force, 40

Library of Congress Cataloging-in-Publication Data

Hatch, Andrew, 1950- author.
  Examining airplane crashes / by Andrew Hatch.
     pages cm – (Examining disasters)
  Includes index.
  Audience: 7-8.
  ISBN 978-1-934545-61-4 (hardcover : alk. paper) – ISBN 978-1-934545-77-5 (ebook)
  1. Aircraft accidents–Juvenile literature. I. Title. II. Series: Examining disasters.
  TL553.5.H386 2015
  363.12'4–dc23
                                                2014044471

Printed in the United States of America
CG1022015

www.oliverpress.com

CONTENTS

ONE

AMERICAN AIRLINES FLIGHT 191

May 25, 1979, was a clear day at Chicago O'Hare International Airport in Illinois. There was visibility of approximately 15 miles (24 km), much greater than the 3-mile (5-km) minimum visibility required for an airplane to take off. American Airlines Flight 191 was scheduled to fly to Los Angeles International Airport in California that day. But what should have been a four-hour-long flight instead ended shortly after takeoff.

The plane was a McDonnell Douglas DC-10 carrying 258 passengers and 13 crew members. This type of airplane has an engine on each wing and one in the tail. As the plane taxied from the gate

Smoke pours from a building after American Airlines Flight 191 crashed into it.

This map shows where Flight 191 crashed after taking off from Chicago O'Hare International Airport.

to the runway, neither the flight crew nor maintenance crew noticed anything wrong. At 3:02 p.m., Flight 191 was cleared for takeoff, and the airplane roared down the runway. As the plane took off, the left engine, pylon assembly, and 3 feet (1 m) of the left wing fell off and landed on the runway. Despite the loss of one of the plane's three engines, the DC-10's wheels left the ground.

At 300 feet (91 m) above the runway, the situation became even worse. The plane rolled to the left until its wings were straight up and down, perpendicular to the ground. Then the plane's nose dipped until it was pointing below the horizon. The plane was in a stall, a situation where an aircraft is moving so slowly that the pilots cannot control it.

At approximately 3:04 p.m., Flight 191 crashed into a field 4,600 feet (1,400 m) northwest of the end of the runway. The wreckage flew into a nearby trailer park. The explosion and fire completely destroyed the airplane, a mobile home, and several cars. All 271 people on the plane were killed, along with two people on the ground nearby. Two other people on the ground were seriously burned.

FLIGHT 191 INVESTIGATIONS

The National Transportation Safety Board (NTSB) is the U.S. government agency that investigates aviation accidents. The NTSB determined an improper maintenance procedure caused the Flight 191 crash. When

ICE

Ice buildup on a plane's wings is one of the most frequent causes of airplane crashes. At high altitudes, ice can build up on a plane's wings and change how air flows over them, potentially causing the plane to stall. Planes have devices on their wings that expand and contract to shatter built-up ice while in flight. When ice builds up on an airplane on the ground, deicing fluid is sprayed over the wings to remove it. Deicing fluid is a mixture of water and a chemical called glycol. Then anti-icing fluid is added to prevent more ice or snow from building up.

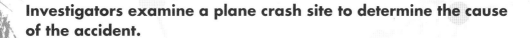

Investigators examine a plane crash site to determine the cause of the accident.

removing an engine for maintenance procedures, proper technique calls for workers to remove the engine first and then remove the pylon assembly. However, American Airlines preferred to remove both the engine and the pylon as a single unit. It saved the company approximately 200 man-hours each time the engine had to be removed. Removing the two pieces together caused the pylon assembly to crack, leading to the failures that caused the crash of Flight 191.

After every airplane crash, investigators work to explain what happened and why. They study each piece of evidence, interview people involved in the accident, and test their hypotheses until they have determined why a crash happened.

Investigations begin at the plane crash site. Parts of the plane are examined and carefully documented. Back in laboratories and offices, investigators study these parts, as well as data from the flight. They carry out

AIR FORCE ONE

No airplanes in the world undergo such strict maintenance checks as Air Force One, the planes that carry the president of the United States. A highly qualified staff closely inspects Air Force One and the runway before each trip. The airplanes also have measures designed to keep them safe from attacks.

Air traffic controllers guide thousands of flights each day to avoid crashes.

tests and run computer simulations. All of the findings are put together to describe the series of events leading up to the disaster, known as the accident chain.

The crash of American Airlines Flight 191 was the deadliest commercial aviation accident in the history of the United States. In response to the crash, American Airlines was fined $500,000 for its improper maintenance procedures. Investigators helped make sure a similar crash would never happen again by putting rules in place to correct the problem.

HOW SCIENCE WORKS

The NTSB, the Federal Aviation Administration (FAA), and sometimes the Federal Bureau of Investigation (FBI) study airplane crashes in the United States. They look at the crash from every possible perspective and study each piece of wreckage to understand exactly what happened. They examine the cockpit voice recorder and flight data recorder. These durable devices, also known as black boxes, record what happens on a flight and are designed to survive crashes. Survivors and witnesses are interviewed, and the plane's flight and maintenance history are reviewed. When the investigation is done, a detailed report is released, including the likely causes of the accident and a list of recommendations to improve safety on future flights.

TWO

FORCES ADD UP

Before discussing how an airplane crashes, it is important to understand how it flies. There are four forces that must be controlled during flight: weight, lift, thrust, and drag. Balancing these forces is what keeps an airplane in the sky. The study of how objects move through air and interact with these forces is known as aerodynamics.

The most obvious force an airplane deals with is weight. Gravity pulls objects toward Earth, giving those objects weight. An airplane must overcome gravity's pull to fly. Because objects with more mass are pulled with more force, larger planes must work harder to overcome gravity.

There are four forces that keep all airplanes in the air.

An airplane's wing shape is designed to create lift.

LIFT AND THRUST

Lift is an upward-pushing force that helps an airplane counteract the downward pull of gravity. When the plane is in motion, the wings' shape causes air to move more quickly over the top than under the bottom of the wings. This speed difference results in lower pressure above the wings, forcing it to move upward into the lower pressure area. Lift makes it possible for airplanes to fly. Pointing a plane up or down changes the way air moves over the wings, increasing or decreasing the amount of lift the wings generate. Lift also changes at different speeds and altitudes.

Like lift, thrust is a pushing force. Airplane engines create thrust to push a plane forward. As a plane moves faster, the air traveling across an airplane's wings also moves faster

FLAPS AND SLATS

Pilots use parts of the wings, called flaps and slats, to change the shape of wings and how they interact with the wind. Flaps on the back of the wings extend downward. This creates lift and drag. Slats are similar to flaps, but they are attached to the front of the wings instead of the back. Both slats and flaps are used during takeoff and landing to create lift or to slow the plane down. Slats and flaps can also be used during flight to steer, if needed.

and increases the lift. When lift is stronger than the pull of gravity, a plane begins to fly.

DRAG

Drag, also known as air resistance, is the fourth force of flight. Air pushes against a plane in the opposite direction of its motion. Airplanes are designed to minimize drag forces. An airplane's smooth surface makes it easier for air to move past the plane, rather than push against it. The more drag a plane encounters, the more thrust it needs to move forward. During landing, pilots use parts of the wings, called flaps, to increase drag, slowing the plane down.

The wrong amount of force at the wrong time can cause accidents. Balancing the four forces is the challenge of safe flight. For American Airlines Flight 191, the plane lost lift as its speed decreased too quickly. The pull of

DECREASING DRAG

Pilots pull an airplane's wheels back into the body of a plane after takeoff. If the wheels were left hanging below the plane, the airplane would experience incredible amounts of drag. The drag would rip the wheels off the plane, because the wheels are not designed to withstand the air pressure created at high speeds.

THE FOUR FORCES

This diagram shows the four forces that act on an airplane. Think about the effect of any of these forces going out of balance. For example, what would happen if the force of thrust increased? How would this affect the other forces?

gravity overpowered the plane and dragged it down into the open field.

THREE

HOW PLANES CRASH

Fatal passenger airliner crashes are incredibly rare. More than 8.7 million airline flights took off within the United States in 2013, and only one had a fatal crash. Crashes happen when the four forces of flight are somehow thrown out of balance. Several different factors can contribute to this imbalance. Design flaws, bad weather, pilot error, and collisions can all lead to a crash.

Even a minor error in the design of an airplane can result in disaster. On October 24, 1947, United Airlines Flight 608 was traveling from Los Angeles to Chicago. The aircraft was a Douglas DC-6, a four-engine plane capable of carrying approximately 100 passengers.

Even the smallest of design errors can force pilots to make an emergency landing or, worse, cause the plane to crash.

THE FIRST PLANE CRASH

Orville and Wilbur Wright designed and built the first airplane in 1903. During a demonstration flight in 1908, Orville Wright lost control of his plane. It crashed nose first from a height of about 100 feet (30 m). Wright had broken bones, but his passenger was not so lucky. He died shortly after. The Wrights learned from the crash and continued to make improvements to their planes.

A few hours into the flight, a fire broke out in the baggage compartment and smoke filled the plane. The pilots tried to land, but the plane crashed on the way to the nearest airport. There were no survivors. Investigators immediately tried to discover what went wrong.

Investigators found the DC-6 had a fuel vent near a device that sucked in air to heat the cabin. If fuel leaked out of the vent, it could get sucked into the heating device. Testing on the ground showed this leak could lead to a fire if it happened while the cabin heater was turned on. After the investigation, all DC-6 aircraft were grounded and modified to prevent another disaster.

BAD WEATHER AND PILOT ERROR

Weather conditions called microbursts are dangerous to airplanes. Microbursts are sudden, powerful gusts of

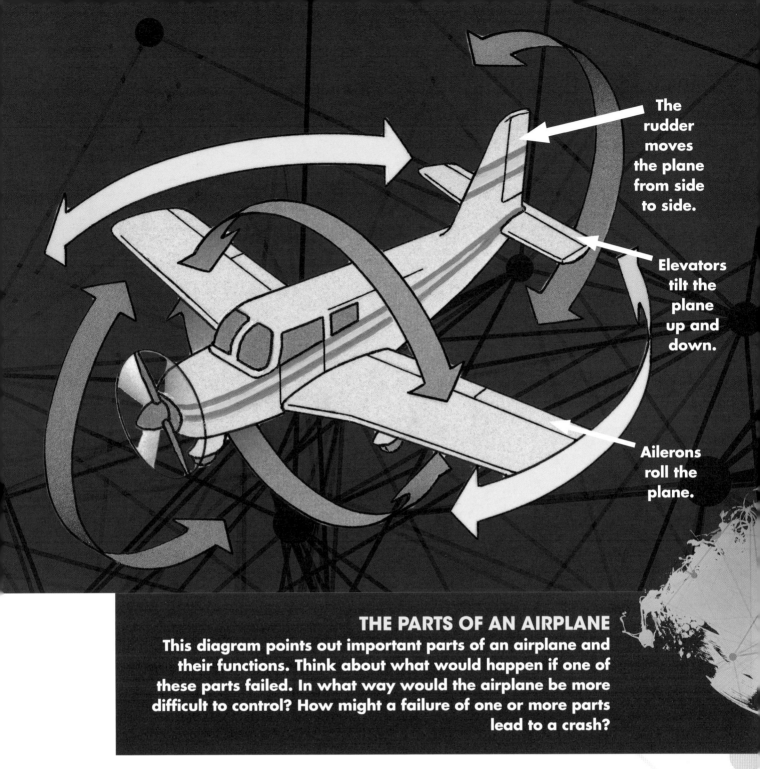

The
rudder
moves
the plane
from side
to side.

Elevators
tilt the
plane
up and
down.

Ailerons
roll the
plane.

THE PARTS OF AN AIRPLANE

This diagram points out important parts of an airplane and their functions. Think about what would happen if one of these parts failed. In what way would the airplane be more difficult to control? How might a failure of one or more parts lead to a crash?

wind that move downward from storm clouds and travel outward when they hit the ground. If microbursts occur during takeoff or landing, the quick shift in winds, known as wind shear, can cause a crash.

An unexpected microburst caused Delta Air Lines Flight 191 to crash in 1985.

A microburst-related crash happened to Delta Air Lines Flight 191 on August 2, 1985. The three-engine Lockheed L-1011 passenger jet was traveling from Fort Lauderdale-Hollywood International Airport in Florida to the Dallas/ Fort Worth International Airport in Texas. As they prepared to land, the pilots noticed potentially dangerous storms in their path but did not try to avoid them. The airplane got caught in a microburst less than 1,000 feet (300 m) above the ground.

The pilots tried to speed up, increase altitude, and fly around for another landing attempt, but it was too late. The plane struck the ground before reaching the runway, hitting a car on a highway and killing the driver. The left wing then hit a structure at the airport, causing the aircraft to spin counterclockwise and explode. Of the 163 people on board, only 27 survived. An investigation showed that the weather conditions, as well as the pilots' failure to avoid the storm, led to the crash.

COLLISIONS

Midair collisions with objects are another cause of plane crashes. The biggest risks happen during

MALAYSIA AIRLINES FLIGHT 370

Sometimes planes crash over the ocean, making it more difficult for investigators to locate the wreckage and determine the cause of the crash. On March 8, 2014, Malaysia Airlines Flight 370 disappeared between Kuala Lumpur, Malaysia, and Beijing, China. It was carrying 227 passengers and 12 crew members. Less than one hour after taking off, Flight 370 stopped communicating with air traffic control and disappeared from radar after appearing to change course. Although it is assumed the plane crashed in a remote area of the Indian Ocean, as of March 2015 the wreckage had not been found.

Passengers from US Airways Flight 1549 wait on the wings for rescue workers to come pick them up.

takeoff and landing. One of the most serious dangers is known as bird strike. This happens when a bird collides with an airplane or gets sucked into an engine. One of the most famous examples of a bird strike happened to US Airways Flight 1549 on January 15, 2009. The airplane involved was a two-engine Airbus A320 jet. The flight was scheduled to travel from New York City to Charlotte, North Carolina.

The journey was cut short minutes into the flight. At around 3,000 feet (900 m), both engines lost power. When a burning smell filled the cockpit, the pilot knew there had been a bird strike. The plane did not have enough thrust to return to the airport, so the pilot aimed for the Hudson River. Airline pilots are trained for water landings, but having to perform one is extremely rare. The pilot of Flight 1549, Chesley Sullenberger, was highly skilled, and he brought the plane down safely. The passengers and crew were soon rescued by nearby boats. No one died.

FOUR

DELIBERATE PLANE CRASHES

Not every plane crash is an accident. Since the beginning of aviation history, terrorists and militaries have recognized the power of using planes as both weapons and targets in war and other conflicts.

A plane can become a weapon if it is hijacked. Some hijackers demand ransom, or money, to land the airplane safely. Others want to crash the plane to make a political point. This includes the terrorists who flew planes into the World Trade Center and the Pentagon on September 11, 2001. These terrorists took flight lessons so they could pilot the planes to their targets. On the day of the attack, they got on their flights, broke

The September 11, 2001, attacks were deliberately carried out by terrorists.

The Martin MB-1 was one of many planes used by the U.S. Army beginning in World War I.

into the cockpits, and took over the controls to carry out their plot.

Since the September 11 attacks, many new safeguards have been put in place to prevent airplane hijackings. Cockpit doors have been strengthened to reinforce them against firearms, knives, and grenades,

and new lock systems have been added so cockpit doors can only be opened from inside the cockpit. Federal Air Marshals, armed guards trained to protect against threats in a plane cabin, were also added to more flights.

PLANES IN WAR

Airplanes came to be a major weapon in warfare during World War I (1914–1918). At first, planes did not carry weapons and were used instead to spy on the enemy. Airplanes, however, were soon equipped with machine guns to fight enemy aircraft. Planes also began carrying bombs that pilots could drop on ground forces. Planes now carry guided missiles and electronic systems designed to hide the airplane from radar detection. With modern jet engines, fighter planes can travel more than twice the speed of sound.

OUTSIDE TARGETS

In addition to being hijacked, commercial airplanes, or planes carrying cargo or passengers, can be shot down from the ground. Sometimes this is a case of mistaken identity, because the shooters may mistake the

HOW SCIENCE WORKS

On July 25, 2000, a supersonic passenger jet called the Concorde burst into flames shortly after taking off from Paris, France. It crashed into a hotel and restaurant, killing 113 people on the plane and the ground combined. The plane's tires burst after hitting debris on the runway, sending pieces of the wheel tearing through fuel lines in the wings. Air France, which operated the flight, grounded the rest of its Concorde airliners while the investigations continued. Investigators made recommendations on how to improve aviation safety in the future based on their findings. Aviation officials and airlines took these recommendations into account before they cleared Concorde jets to resume flying.

Debris from Flight MH17 lays smoking after it was believed to have been shot down by pro-Russian separatists in Ukraine.

commercial plane for a military aircraft. This may have happened when Malaysia Airlines Flight MH17 crashed over Ukraine on July 17, 2014, likely shot down by pro-Russian separatists. These rebels were fighting against

AERIAL REFUELING

The distance a plane can fly is limited by how much fuel it can carry. Fighter jets use a large amount of fuel. With modern technology, some planes can refuel in the air. If they had to, these aircraft could fly indefinitely. Big planes, called aerial tankers, carry thousands of gallons of fuel. To refuel, a fighter jet flies next to the aerial tanker. The two planes must maintain the same speed. A long tube called a flying boom connects the tanker to the jet. The flying boom transfers up to 6,000 pounds (2,700 kg) of fuel per minute. When the transfer is complete, the smaller jet detaches and goes on its way with a full tank of fuel.

the Ukrainian government and were likely armed by Russia. The crash killed 283 passengers and 15 crew members. A missile fired from an SA-11 antiaircraft missile battery likely shot down Flight MH17. Messages on social media following the attack appeared to show that separatists believed the Malaysia Airlines flight was a Ukrainian military plane. The separatists lacked the proper equipment and training that would have helped them distinguish between a military and civilian aircraft.

After that tragedy, the Federal Aviation Administration (FAA) created a no-fly zone over eastern Ukraine. Usually, airlines monitor security situations on the ground and decide their own flight paths.

A U.S. Air Force plane lines up with an aerial tanker over the skies of Afghanistan.

Malaysia Airlines continued to fly over Ukraine despite it being a war zone. The U.S. government can mandate no-fly zones and prohibit flight paths that cross those areas.

FLIGHT
RECORDER
DO NOT OPEN

FIVE

STOPPING THE ACCIDENT CHAIN

On June 1, 2009, Air France Flight 447 headed toward a monster thunderstorm. The flight would soon go on record as France's deadliest air disaster. The accident chain began when the plane flew directly into the storm over the Atlantic Ocean. The plane's wings became covered in ice, causing it to lose lift. A device that prevents stalls stopped working, and the aircraft went into a fatal stall and crashed into the ocean. When the plane's black boxes were finally recovered two years later, the cause of the accident became clear. The crash was a combination of pilot error, lack of training, and equipment malfunction. These issues, like those of most

Two years after Flight 447 crashed, its flight boxes were found in the Atlantic Ocean. This helped investigators determine the cause of the crash.

FLIGHT SIMULATORS

Pilots must complete many training hours inside a simulator, a model cockpit with realistic controls. Instead of windows, it uses computer screens to show what a pilot would see during a real flight. Some simulators sit on supports that allow them to move, giving them the feel of an actual flight. A simulator operator, who controls the simulator, sits at a computer station. He or she can program different flight situations into the simulator, giving the pilot a chance to train for many different situations.

plane crashes, are preventable or avoidable.

CHECKING THE WEATHER

Weather can usually be predicted, and pilots are trained to avoid certain kinds of severe weather. Airports sometimes delay flights during bad storms. Pilots review weather patterns before every takeoff, studying weather maps carefully. Most violent weather is located close to the ground. Ice, snow, slush, sleet, and wind bursts can usually be avoided at higher altitudes. Improved training and warning systems also help pilots handle weather problems. Still, weather can change without notice, and turbulence can be a problem at cruising altitude. Cruising altitude is the height at which a plane requires the least amount of fuel to fly. Cruising

altitudes can be as high as 39,000 feet (12,000 m) for commercial airliners. Airplanes spend approximately 57 percent of their flight time at their cruising altitude between ascent and descent.

SATELLITE TRACKING

The disappearance of Malaysia Airlines Flight 370 renewed the demand for satellite tracking of commercial aircraft so that their locations would be known in the event of a crash. The technology to do this exists, but so far has not been widely used due to its cost. Satellite tracking could allow faster recovery of black boxes from crash sites, helping to determine the cause of a crash more quickly. Most commercial planes have beacons that transmit their location in the event of an emergency. Since the crash of Flight 370, the call for flight recorders that stream real-time flight data via satellite has grown stronger.

PILOT REVIEW

Before every flight, pilots review other details besides the weather. They walk around their aircraft to check for any issues on the plane's hull and other parts. Pilots check the

A pilot runs through his preflight checklist before takeoff.

plane's weight and balance to ensure the airplane will
have enough thrust and lift for flight. They use checklists
to complete the correct steps for takeoff and landing. This
attention to detail helps make air travel extremely safe.

An aircraft's safety wires are inspected for any issues.

Planes also have backup systems that help avoid problems. But, with hundreds of switches, instruments, and warning lights in the cockpit, pilots have to keep track of a great deal. It's very rare, but sometimes systems fail. Even with all their training, pilots can miss warnings. Some air travel experts believe pilots are becoming overly dependent upon automatic systems. These experts feel pilots need additional training on how to fly without these systems.

People have been flying for more than a century. Since the first flights, aircraft designers and pilots have

HOW SCIENCE WORKS

The de Havilland Comet was the first commercial jet airliner. Introduced in 1952, the plane could fly higher and faster than most other planes of its time. Every airline wanted one. Then, a series of fatal crashes affected the future of jet airliners. Investigators blamed each crash on a different problem. Finally, the planes were grounded. Investigators decided to try reconstructing one of them from the broken pieces to discover why it crashed. This technique had never been used before. It became clear that each crash had resulted from the same problem. Unlike other airplanes, jet aircraft fly at high altitudes, where the air is thin. The jets must be sealed off and filled with thicker air to make the aircraft comfortable for the passengers inside. This process is called pressurization. Each pressurization weakens the plane's metal body, similar to how a metal paper clip weakens when you bend it repeatedly. The weakening process is known as metal fatigue. Scientists learned more about metal fatigue from the accidents, and they changed the design of jet aircraft to make them stronger.

needed to understand the forces that allow planes to move through the air. Engineers and scientists study every accident with these forces in mind. After more than 100 years of learning about how planes can fail, the major problems have been fixed, making it more difficult than ever before to find the causes of plane crashes. Investigators must look at every detail of the flight, studying and testing every possibility until they find the answer. Thanks to people who investigate crashes, every accident that happens leads to improvements in flight safety.

CASE STUDY

INVESTIGATING FLIGHT 427

When USAir Flight 427 crashed near Pittsburgh, Pennsylvania, on September 8, 1994, 132 people died. The NTSB began an investigation immediately. Many people believed the rudder system had failed. The rudder allows a plane to change its side-to-side direction. The power control unit (PCU) that controls the rudder was taken apart and inspected piece by piece. No problems were found.

Investigators met to look at the evidence again in 1996. They thought the PCU might have failed because of cold temperatures during flight. Tests were run using the same temperatures found at high altitudes. The PCU from Flight 427 was tested alongside a brand-new one. During the tests, the PCU kept jamming while the new one worked. The investigation showed thorough testing could reveal the causes of crashes, even if they were minor.

TOP TEN WORST AIRPLANE CRASHES

1. **SEPTEMBER 11, 2001, NEW YORK CITY; WASHINGTON, DC; PENNSYLVANIA, UNITED STATES**

   Terrorists piloted two planes into the World Trade Center in New York City and one into the Pentagon near Washington, DC. A fourth plane crashed in a field in Pennsylvania when its passengers tried to retake the plane. These terrorist attacks killed 2,977 people.

2. **MARCH 27, 1977, TENERIFE, CANARY ISLANDS**

   When two Boeing 747 jumbo jets crashed into each other on the runway, a total of 583 passengers and crew members were killed.

3. **AUGUST 12, 1985, MOUNT TAKAMAGAHARA, JAPAN**

   A Boeing 747 had a mechanical error that sent it crashing into Mount Takamagahara. A total of 520 people died in the deadliest single-aircraft accident in history.

4. **NOVEMBER 12, 1996, NEAR NEW DELHI, INDIA**

   Shortly after departing, Saudi Arabian Airlines Flight 763 crashed into incoming Kazakhstan Airlines Flight 1907. A total of 349 victims died in the deadliest midair collision in history.

5. MARCH 3, 1974, BOIS D'ERMENONVILLE, FRANCE

A chain of events that began when a faulty rear cargo hatch blew off ended with an out-of-control plane. Turkish Airlines Flight 981 crashed near Paris, France, killing all 346 people on board.

6. JUNE 23, 1985, OFF THE COAST OF IRELAND

Sikh extremists sabotaged Air India Flight 182. The crash killed all 329 passengers and crew en route from Toronto to London.

7. AUGUST 19, 1980, RIYADH, SAUDI ARABIA

Flight 163 caught fire shortly after taking off. The plane made an emergency landing after smoke was reported. But an emergency evacuation was not ordered, and the 301 passengers and crew died of smoke inhalation.

8. JULY 17, 2014, HRABOVE, UKRAINE

Malaysia Airlines Flight MH17 was shot down near the Ukrainian village of Hrabove after being mistaken for a Ukrainian military aircraft, killing all 298 people on board.

9. JULY 2, 1988, PERSIAN GULF

A U.S. Navy ship shot down Iran Air Flight 655 after mistaking it for a military aircraft. All 290 passengers and crew were killed.

10. FEBRUARY 19, 2003, SHAHDAD, IRAN

Two hundred and seventy-five military personnel died when a military plane crashed in southern Iran due to poor weather conditions, including high winds and fog.

GLOSSARY

ALTITUDE: Height above the ground.

CABIN: The inside of an airplane.

COCKPIT: The section of an aircraft in which the pilots sit.

ENGINEERS: People who use math and science to design things and solve problems.

HIJACK: To take over a plane or other vehicle by force.

HULL: The main body of an airplane.

HYPOTHESES: Ideas or theories that are not proven but that lead to further study.

PYLON ASSEMBLY: The structure that connects a DC-10's engine to its wing.

RUDDER: A control surface at the rear of a plane that is used to control the plane's direction.

RUNWAY: A flat surface on which airplanes take off and land.

SIMULATIONS: Tests that represent the conditions likely to happen during a real flight.

STALL: A situation in which there is not enough air traveling over an airplane's wings to generate the lift needed to stay in the air.

TAXI: A plane's movement along the ground on its wheels.

TURBULENCE: An air condition that can cause bumpy flights.

FURTHER INFORMATION

BOOKS

Berliner, Don. *Aviation: Reaching for the Sky*. Minneapolis: The Oliver Press, Inc., 1997.

Lusted, Marcia Amidon. *Surviving Accidents and Crashes*. Minneapolis: Lerner Publications, 2008.

Woods, Michael and Mary B. Woods. *Air Disasters*. Minneapolis: Lerner Publications, 2008.

WEBSITES

http://www.grc.nasa.gov/WWW/k-12/BGA/BGAindex.html
This website features interesting information on all aspects of aerodynamic activities.

http://howthingsfly.si.edu
This website has videos and animations that show how the forces of flight work.

INDEX